PAINTED WORDS

POETRY, ART AND PARKINSON'S

·

CHANTAL
WOLF

One Printers Way
Altona, MB R0G 0B0
Canada

www.friesenpress.com

Copyright © 2022 by Chantal Wolf
First Edition — 2022

Author photo by Jaime Churchward of JY Photography. www.jyphotography.org

All rights reserved.

No part of this publication may be reproduced in any form, or by any means, electronic or mechanical, including photocopying, recording, or any information browsing, storage, or retrieval system, without permission in writing from FriesenPress.

ISBN
978-1-03-915334-9 (Hardcover)
978-1-03-915333-2 (Paperback)
978-1-03-915335-6 (eBook)

1. POETRY, SUBJECTS & THEMES, WOMEN AUTHORS

Distributed to the trade by The Ingram Book Company

PAINTED WORDS

POETRY, ART AND PARKINSON'S

for the poets, the artists, the makers, all those who bravely
speak their own language of creativity and for those
who have yet to discover their voice.

My Journey through Paint and Poetry

I love the silence of the early morning, the comforting stillness. It feels open and safe—outstretched arms ready to dance with the simmering possibilities that float around my groggy, not fully awake head. I turn on the light in my studio—my sacred space—where each day is filled with a joyful connection to the creative process.

Calling myself an artist, uncovering my artist's voice, having a studio space—at one time all of this seemed like a distant dream. A dream which only briefly saw the light of day before being buried beneath doubt and insecurity, indecision, marriage, kids, careers, divorce—life.

Long before the layers of "life" happened, I remember a little girl, about four years old, posing for a family photo with her younger sister in matching red raincoats—a last snapshot before leaving our UK home and boarding a flight to Canada.

After a smooth transition to life in Toronto, my childhood continued, mostly happily—plenty of time spent outdoors discovering my corner of the world. It was an active season of creative, artful expression fuelled by a sense of freedom, curiosity and a busy imagination, unaffected by the adolescent angst yet to come.

Somewhere in my late teens, I got small. I lost my way. I lost my way before I even knew what my way was. The voices around me grew louder as mine became very quiet. I thought they knew better, I thought they knew the way—and I wasn't brave enough to envision any other path. So, I focused my energy on moulding and shaping, what I thought would be, a preferred and more pleasing version of me.

Choices were made—to step off the creative path after art college for a "safer, more sensible" clerical job, to marry a man I thought I could "fix." I became a mom. I did my best, but I was young, I let feelings of discontent and unease distract me from fully showing up. Eventually the marriage ended and I steered my way through single parenthood for the next few years— back in my childhood home under my parents' roof—with my kids. Not an easy dynamic to navigate. It often meant having to twist and contort myself in imaginative ways.

At the same time, I began to sift through the mind-made rubble, hoping to unearth long buried fragments of myself. I dug deeper fumbling to find more parts that felt true. I read books by the wise and the knowing. I found a renewed sense of purpose through my work in special education. I felt called to draw and paint again. It was an ongoing process of releasing and revealing, rooting out the solid pieces of myself—pieces that were ready to welcome new love and marriage to a man whose generous loving heart and boundless support continue to nurture and hold me through this journey.

Then, in 2016, I was diagnosed with Parkinson's Disease.

Not the most pleasant diagnosis, but not the worst. And surprisingly, not a huge shock either. Parkinson's is a progressive disease that holds plenty of challenges. I was already well-acquainted with some of them—like the tremors, poor balance, painful, rigid muscles, the feeble scribble that was once lovely handwriting—the list goes on.

Although I didn't choose this, I decided early on I could choose how to respond. Rather than letting worry and uncertainty be the driving forces, I wanted art and creativity to lead the way. Not to say that fear doesn't hover nearby, because it does. I am most likely in for a bumpy ride ahead. But for now, I see this diagnosis as a bright pink permission slip, a loud YES telling me to crack open the lid of my own creative ideas. I had things to say that needed to get out!

Over the years, in between work and family life, I'd kept my skills sharp with commissioned drawings, paintings, portraits, and murals. But, I was often creating art to fit someone else's expectations. I wanted to make art that was authentically my own. Since then, it's been a wild ride on the "magical mystery tour" of creativity. I have embraced a daily painting practice, slowed down to listen while my intuitive inner artist finds her voice, and paid close attention to the sparks of joy and curiosity. Along the way, some interesting surprises have emerged. Like finding lost treasure—I discovered the rich and wondrous world of poetry. Not an entirely new discovery, but I had no idea the profound impact it would have in my life.

Much of this happened as Covid-19 began its global sweep and essentially banished everyone to their room—or studio, as the case may be. When the pared down life felt too isolated, even for this introvert, I found connection with an online community of artists, makers, and creatives. These extraordinary women have inspired and empowered me in countless meaningful ways. In particular, by shining a light on the magic of poetry. Not the obscure poetry I tried to make sense of in school, but an expansive new language—like art with words.

Finding poetry, reading poetry, listening to poetry, sinking into poetry, and now writing poetry has been transformative. A gift. Speaking the language of poetry and art—painting with words—feels revolutionary. I am awakening a voice that reaches deep within the tender truths of being human and gently whispers them into existence.

Waking up my voice, my artist's voice, my poet's voice—exposing the raw sensitive underbelly of me— is both terrifying and exhilarating. This book is an intimate excavation of the raw and the sensitive. Through poetry, I celebrate, examine, reflect. I dig for insights, try to make sense of the senseless, and honour the beauty in the mystery.

Come. Walk with me through these pages as I share from my heart, the language of the soul.

painted words • the poems

edges	1
the process	3
within	6
being me	8
too much in my head	9
speak what's inside	11
behind the paint	14
from the bones	16
twenty-twenty	18
swimming in mud	20
time	22
home	24
seven sisters	26
ode to October	28
wintry days	29
the shape of love	31
unearthed	33
now that you're not here	34
be like a tree	36
optimism	38
three thoughts behind	40
I see you	42
that day in November	44
not today	46
fading away	49

edges

clutching the intimately familiar
content to remain on the shore
where the water meets the sand and the rock
of cautious, sensitive me
the caress of each wave
gently washing away the difficult knotted edges
the ones that define and confine
parked on the perimeter
looking in, listening in, leaning in
watching for sparks that ignite and excite
the drowsy and the dormant
to push past what's long been guarded, protected
but now lays in a jumbled up heap
on the outskirts of hushed hesitation
how do I reassemble the sense, or the meaning
to speak of its valid existence?
lost and unsure I return to the edges that feel inseparable,
a devoted extension of me

the edges I create with paint and brush,
edges I reach for with practice and play,
edges I nudge and trust to expand,
the hard edges, the soft, faint and bold,
the unclear, confident, blended, and blurred,
the weak, watery, sharp and strong
a lifetime straddling the border of back and forth
coyly flirting with the balance
between watchful wallflower and insecure guest

but these edges are mine, I am the guardian, keeper and curator
of the meticulously crafted, well-tended and cared for
threaded with curiosity, weaved with attention
inside, delicate slivers of insight, shards of clarity
hand selected and placed just so
awaiting that awkward moment
when the spotlight catches an edge of its inviting glow.

the process

swirling images
overflowing thoughts
what waits to breathe?
what will rise from the unlit?
what conversations will murmur and chatter?
chasing inspiration like fireflies
sparks that scurry and scoot, flicker and flash
trailing after the fleeting and elusive
fighting the urge to imitate, replicate

who is speaking? my head? my hand? my heart?

go beyond the muddied mind
through weighty, stifling analysis
the judgements, the lessons, the rules
past the landfill of "should" and "must"
sidestepping the fears that try their best to be the boss
distractions, diversions abound, demanding attention
more loudly than the art
but listen close to the whispers
the faint quiet inklings, that want only to exist
feel them flutter and awaken
all bleary eyed and foggy
looking around for the light

feel the pull of curiosity
of wonder and of awe
of freedom mixed with astonishment,
take them firmly by the hand
they will lead you to the gifts unopened
yet clearly addressed to you

soak in the essence of these gifts
immerse your fingers in the paint
watch the watery dance of pigment
glide along a paper surface
fill your brush with luscious colour

or your page with juicy words
move your body to the music playing bravely in your head
sing your song as only you can
no matter if it comes out
a little off-key
just honest and open
somewhat messily imperfect

created to create
something breathed from nothing
the miracle exists
to shape and share
our many human ways to be.

within

a space born of questions
delicious questions
inviting luscious pause
juicy, full-bodied, robust questions

questions to nudge, to nurture
to chase the curious inklings
wade beyond the bleak and barren
come swim in the deep waters, they call

lean into these questions
dive within, below the surface
the answers may remain elusive
just dare to sink into unknowns

as the questions ripple out across the miles
reaching those who speak—
with a paint-filled brush,
the snap of a lens,
through threads of contemplation
or the tender words, scribed along a page

we shelter, in this space
a radical safe haven
of creative hands
making from the raw and true
as we unwrap the shards of broken glass we carry
together

witness to the wisdom rising from our wounds
and nourished by the questions unfolding from
within.

being me

how do I be me?
when me is fading
when me is shaking
when me is changing
when me is slowing
when me is different
when the pavement ends

I know how to be me today
all the parts still make sense
but will they tomorrow, when nothing is clear?
how do I get it right? I want to get it right.
who decides what's right? —what does right even look like?
and do I have what it takes?
what if I'm not brave enough, strong enough, resilient enough?
is my sense of humour intact? —definitely going to need that
don't want to take myself too seriously
she says, while examining the weighty, dismal and dark
what if I lose me—lose pieces I've only just found?
detour ahead, recalculating, signals scrambled
proceed to the route and check the map—where is the map? —is there a map?
I really wish there was a map or at least an informative guidebook,
a step-by-step on YouTube perhaps, a Masterclass or TED talk

I know how to be me today, but will I tomorrow?
even as I spill these questions liberally across the page
do I really know this "me"
today or tomorrow, after all?
yet the way life unfolds moment by moment
reminds me that the process of "being me" will evolve much the same
I can't plan it out in advance
nor pre-write the script, the scenes or the acts, in this unfamiliar play
instead I'll reshape and revise the rough outline
as the framework begins to shift
and store some faith in my back pocket
that all will be okay.

too much in my head

where are the words?
I try to grab hold
of the fragments of thoughts, phrases, feelings
orbiting the clutter

a disorganized, overused mess
of the to-do lists, the wonderings, the worries and the vague creative inklings
amidst the self-imposed, self-directed, self-judging pressure to keep up

it's all just a murky pool of mind-made muck

a myriad of pondering to stir around and analyze
sift through the many scripts
for transgressions and infractions
coz' there's bound to be a few
of the "coulda," "shoulda," "wouldas" that rear their ugly heads

but what's said is said,
it's done and dusted, finito and kaput
move on, dear mind

—there's really nothing much to see here any more.

speak what's inside

just speak what's inside
pleads your unpracticed teen voice
silently submerged
as you dab the glistening evidence
of longings and belongings
shoved under the pillow
of rocks
just speak what's inside they said back then
we're tired of the game of guess
what's resting in between the lost and the found
the confined and fiercely defended
but you wore the burden of perfection like skin
stretched much too tight
to ever commit to naming things
hiding beneath those rocks,
without first being shed
of the need to be understood

just speak—it sounds so simple
to those who know the language
of the fast talking, word savvy
verbal entrepreneur
who doesn't think twice about leaving
the room devoid of air

but your language doesn't have to live in that airless place—
it waits in the idle pause, before each inhale
hovering in the brushes of watery blue
within the trembling marks made true
a clumsy dance of thoughts
with their own
peculiar rhythm

just speak your imperfect language
however disorderly and jumbled
speak from the core of raw within
and release what passes for approval
because somewhere in the midst
of alive and aloud
the words
might
simply
drop
away.

behind the paint

what will they see
when all of it is fresh?

will they see the layer upon layer upon layer
of each ugly messy effort?
will they feel the weight of lofty well-meant intentions?
hear the bickering debate carrying on in my head?
mostly scattered thoughts and focus,
questions I hesitate to ask,
hours and hours and hours that refuse to be counted
can they be seen by the naked eye?

will they touch the prickly brushstrokes that remain
after misguided attempts at correcting
what was likely just fine in the first place

smoke and mirrors, paint and promise
don't you know?
a paintbrush wielding fraud, pretending skills I may not have

but before I sink too deep into a swamp of expectations
swallowed by the need to get it right
I ask, what is it you want to say?
that doesn't live in words
but speaks in crisp green and gentle blue
through delicate meandering lines
that flow, into marks demanding and bold
telling tales of doubt and regret, of strength and resolve

the secrets laid bare, exposed, on display
rising from underneath the mud
brushed and blended by hands unsteady yet determined
to paint the lightness of each emerging truth.

from the bones

these bones speak when the voice is mute
these bones feel what the words find conflicted
these bones hold the truth, untold and unshared

swirling and spinning deep in the marrow
as if caught in a tide pool
of hushed consideration

my worth assessed by the chatter of others
all the rulings, the findings and multitude of conclusions
where I see myself lacking
held captive in these bones

what will it take to free these notions
from their judgemental restraint?
to loosen the core of sinuous threads
that weaken these bones
and choke their speech

but these bones are stable and resilient enough
to bear the full accumulated weight
that remains after sifting through
all the rubbish and debris

leaving space for languages varied and open
choices of how to express
from the deep core of these bones
all that must be freed.

twenty-twenty

2020—perfect vision
the repeating numbers suggest
but we didn't see this coming
caught unaware as we were, mostly
of the sickness
that crept across the planet
in more ways
than we keep
our eyes open to see
the twists in the plot
which can be found on page three
of the plans made in advance
of a time when we thought nothing
of being in a crowd
of people
in public
in a space or a place
to cheer the performance
with the audience of many
to clink glasses on the patio
after admiring the brushstrokes up close
in the gallery
of what might just be possible
or take in the film
just released
in the theatre across town
the simple delights of sharing with others
the food, the music, the company—the embrace
—cancelled until further notice

stay home, stay safe, stay apart, stay sane, somehow—
compressed as we are into our boxes
that feel like coffins
as the day melts one into the other into the other
the blur of life half lived
on the edge of fear and falling apart

"we're all in this together"
declares the sign in front
of the school down the street
that sits empty
together yet separate

a non-contact sport
six feet apart, two metres as we say in the north
marked on the floor where you stand
with your smile submerged and your oh so clean cart
full enough to feed a small city
that has retreated inside to wait out the intruder
who we'd hoped
would have taken their leave
by the time
the landscape traded its grey winter jacket
for a pop of colour

yet here we are
one year in this historical blip
a virus wreaking havoc
across the planet
still holding us captive as we wait
for the shot in the arm
that might free us
to take a step closer
to each other
in person
in union and reunion
of gratitude
for simply being alive
and together.

swimming in mud

swimming in the mud
of gloomy grey words
weighed down by the
heavy and cumbersome

where are breezy light thoughts and ideas
all feather soft and weightless
stripped of any possible harm
from their sharp or offensive edges?

searching in vain
for the delicate words
hoping to grasp a hold
but, like a breath of fairy dust
quite impossible to capture and contain

why does it feel like the balance is off?
as dense clouds sink into bruises and dents
broadcast across tongues, the residue spreads
little air left open for passions to speak

rivals and teammates; these assorted thoughts
can we meet in the middle, perhaps?
somewhere between gently uplifted
and a whole heap of worry
because it might be time to drag myself
out of this thick, insidious mud.

time

this time, next time, sometime, whenever you have time,
the wrong time, the right time—when is that exactly?
no time like the present, time for this, time for that,
free time, my time, your time, playtime, overtime,
kid time, fun time, adult time, swim time, one time in band camp—

a moment in time, the race against time, the time has come
time waits for no man—what about a woman?

pacific time, central, eastern and atlantic
lunchtime, dinnertime, anytime
is now the time?

—the time for what?
if not now, then when?

for this time, this lifetime
can feel fleetingly fast
speeding on by before we can blink

so the question arises,
how will we spend this time, our time?
—this unknown quantity
allotted for us?

home

two hours north of the concrete cage
two years north of reclaiming delight and wonder
a journey back to remembering
the anticipation of the not yet worn
a feeling of home that
rests deep in my bones
on this day in June that holds all the light

the frail exposed edges are starting to curl
of things tender and unfinished
that I trapped and dragged home
like the falling leaf
that knew when to let go
these bones know the truth
on this day in June that holds all the light

the air obligingly fresh and sweet
nourishing all once awash with shadows
as my awkward, unsteady pace
falls into rhythm along well-trodden trails
whispering songs of the stones, of the soil
these bones are rooted
on this day in June that holds all the light

drawing close to the water's edge
its changing moods offer a familiar embrace
a pulse of restless, quiet, steady, then still
gently guiding me back to the source
these bones are alive
on this day in June that holds all the light

two years north of leaving hard urban edges
for this softer simpler life
learning to listen and to breathe
with the seasons of the earth
these bones are blessed
these bones are home
on this day in June that holds all the light.

seven sisters

still standing, for now
stately giants reaching ever skyward
for an intimate date with the clouds
a chorus line of leafless limbs
linked in solidarity, this group of seven
half a generation spent in silent witness
to the rhythm of life unfolding below
oh to imagine what they've seen from their heights
the comings and goings of seasons and storms,
school days and snow days,
sunsets and secrets
what is it that they're feeling now?
all defenseless and exposed
their summer wardrobe stripped away
gowns of lavish green, scattered by the wind

casualties alas, of a small ravenous bug
all jewel toned and brilliant
on a single-minded mission of ash tree demolition
programmed to destroy
slowly feasting its way through
the forest's buffet,
into backyards and woodlots
across rivers and borders
craftily ambushing Mother Nature's bounty
with no foe armed nor prepared
to take on this tiny invader

so when all hopes appear dashed
for an extension, a reprieve
to appreciate their noble presence
at least until autumn
the seven sisters wait
for the day that has no numbers
only to be shattered by a nap busting buzz
as it slices decisively through the still morning air.

ode to October

dear October,
you got it all going on—
with a flair for the sensational,
sassy and bold
radiant, gently confident
often envied
always admired
her story ever-changing
from the fallen and dishevelled
sprinkled underfoot
to the fiery earth tones
trending far above
crisp breezes whisper shivers across your skin
tickling the indigo water
before her gracious waltz
through an orchestra of trees
dear October,
you are where I long to linger
like the woodsmoke that wants to snuggle
into the weave of my wool sweater
yet she doesn't hold too tightly
to those fleeting autumn treasures
dear October,
you understand the rhythms
and the rhymes that
flirt and dance through seasons
over distances and time
how nothing is ever permanent
and the beauty is in the honouring
whatever your "right now" holds
before that very moment
when letting go is all
you really have to do.

wintry days

oh the impartial tones of
winter's muted palette
hues of grey, slate, umber
stark, peeled back, exposed
humbly naked and undressed

crumbled reminders of autumn
have all but disappeared
stirred and scattered
like the seasonings added
to a nourishing earthy soup
—here in this forest kitchen
where nothing ever goes to waste

reduce, reuse, recycle, you heard it here first
the revolving world of life, death, rebirth and renewal
streaming live in a natural space near you
—watch for the upcoming
springtime performance

but first, a moment to marvel at how
trillions of tiny intricate flakes
can assemble a show to rival all others
this masterful collection of exquisite wee treasures
all painted white and sparkly
—lest we forget the existence of the
mystifying and magical

like an interlude played softly between the changing scenes
these days, undecided
find me cocooned in stillness
sifting through the tranquil soil
for cues and intentions
dreams and schemes and gems of aspirations
waiting among the dusky shadows
of a timid and weary sun.